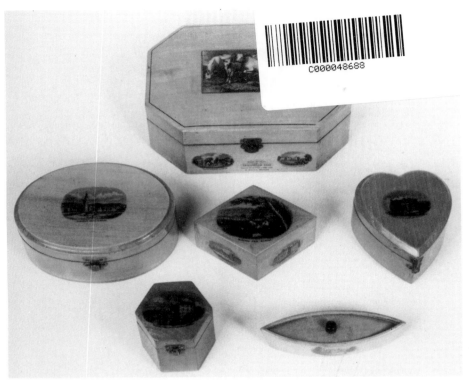

Boxes of every shape and size, with views in transfer ware. Top: Octagonal jewel box with scenes associated with the white cattle at Chillingham Park. Centre: Oval box (Ambleside church and school). Diamond box (mineral well, Moffat). Heart shape box (Golden Lion Hotel, Hunstanton). Bottom: Small hexagonal box (Old Putney Bridge and toll house). Canoe shape (Dunkeld Cathedral).

MAUCHLINE WARE
and Associated Scottish Souvenir Ware

John Baker

Shire Publications Ltd

CONTENTS

Published in 1998 by Shire Publications Ltd, Cromwell House, Church Street, Princes Risborough, Buckinghamshire HP27 9AA, UK.

Printed in Great Britain by CIT Printing Services, Press Buildings, Merlins Bridge, Haverfordwest, Pembrokeshire SA61 1XF.

British Library Cataloguing in Publication Data. Baker, John. Mauchline ware and associated Scottish souvenir ware. — (Shire albums; 140). 1. Mauchline ware. I. Title. 745.594 NK9645.M3. ISBN 0-85263-734-9.

ACKNOWLEDGEMENTS

The author wishes to record his thanks to all those who provided encouragement and information, including Mrs E. Smith and Miss E. Smith, Mr B. Lambie, Mr W. Gray, Dr G. and Mrs D. Scoular and Mr J. Laurenson, all of Scotland, and Mr R. de Peyer, Mrs S. Cordell, Mrs E. Riley, Mrs J. Pollitt, Miss D. Fisher, Mrs S. Thompson and in particular Dr G. Harrison, through whose generosity Mauchline ware may be viewed in Leeds; also Margaret Berriman and Barbara Baker for typing the manuscript. The photographs on the following pages are by K. B. Photographics of Cheltenham: pages 1, 3, 4, 5, 7, 8, 9, 10, 12 (upper), 13 (upper), 14 (lower), 15, 16, 17, 18, 19, 20, 21, 32.

COVER: *A representative selection of most Mauchline ware finishes. Tartan items comprise a 'Caledonia' tartan egg etui, a 'Stuart' tartan ribbon container and a 'Murray' tartan letter opener. Fern ware is represented by a spill vase and a spherical wool or string holder. The novelty wheelbarrow has photographic views of Freshwater in the Isle of Wight and the black lacquer box has a sentimental verse in a floral surround. The 'Burns' book, cenotaph thermometer, large egg in cup, match holder plane, cylindrical match holder and Jubilee box are all in transfer ware. The final item is a snuff box with red ink decoration.*

BELOW: *An advertisement from Menzies' Tourist Pocket Guide for Scotland, 1852. Note the wide range of plane tree items (Mauchline ware) available at the time.*

Darning mushrooms. 'Bottle' shape with Herne Bay view (transfer). From left: Largs from the pier (transfer). Wish Tower, Eastbourne (transfer). Blackpool Tower (photographic).

INTRODUCTION

Some 11 miles (18 km) inland from the Scottish coastal resort of Ayr lies the small town of Mauchline — pronounced 'Moch'lin'. When passing through the town today, it is difficult to appreciate that this was the centre of an industry which in its heyday in the 1860s employed some four hundred people in the manufacture of small but always beautifully made and invariably useful wooden souvenirs and gift ware. Not only were Mauchline's products sold throughout the United Kingdom but vast quantities were exported to many parts of Europe, North America, South Africa, Australia and probably elsewhere. Very similar products were made in other locations, notably Lanark, but so dominant was the contribution of the Mauchline firm of W. and A. Smith that, irrespective of the source of manufacture, the vast range of wooden souvenirs produced in south-west Scotland from the early years of the nineteenth century until the 1930s is now referred to by the generic name of 'Mauchline ware'.

If it were not for the town's association with Robert Burns it would be difficult to find any present-day connection with the industry which provided employment for the bulk of the town's workforce for over a century. Mauchline's Burns House Museum does, however, include an excellent collection of the products of W. and A. Smith as well as commemorating the local poet. The factory itself, known locally as the Box Works, was badly damaged by fire in 1933, this date effectively marking the end of production of the lines for which the firm was so well known. The site is now occupied by Mauchline fire station.

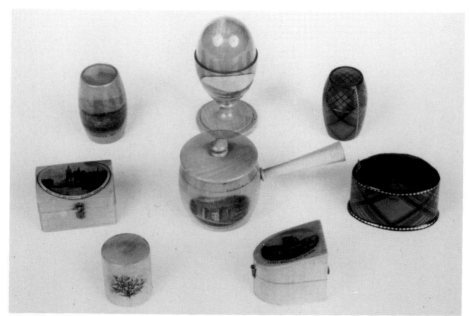

ABOVE: *Novelty thimble containers. Back: Barrel, Freshwater Bay, Isle of Wight (transfer). Egg in egg cup. Lamlash from the pier (photographic). Barrel ('McDuff' tartan). Centre: Chest, Aberdeen market cross (photographic). Saucepan, Castle Menzie, Aberfeldy (transfer). Oval ('Stuart' tartan). Front: Cylinder with 'Forget me not' cartouche. Miniature knife box, Laxey Wheel, Isle of Man (transfer).*

BELOW: *'Egg' etuis (sewing companions). Back: 'Seaweed'. The Chain Pier, Brighton (transfer). Fern. 'Prince Charlie' tartan. Front: Egg opened to reveal its contents. The transfer view is of the Grass Market and Castle, Edinburgh.*

Snuff boxes incorporating the integral hidden hinge. Top, Scarborough (transfer). Centre: Cockerel and hen with the cryptic caption 'Gratis' (hand-painted). 'Come away do — what are you staring at?' (transfer). Two-horse trap (pen and ink work). Bottom: 'When shall we three meet again?' (transfer). Bantam (hand-painted). Note that the last box is no larger than a 2p piece. This box also has the stamp of 'SMITH - MAUCHLINE' on the tinning. Makers names are not decipherable on the other boxes. Some of the captions show a risqué Victorian sense of humour.

THE ORIGINS

Mauchline ware developed partly by accident and partly through necessity. Towards the end of the eighteenth century in the town of Alyth, Perthshire (now Tayside), there lived a man of remarkable inventiveness by the name of John Sandy. Sandy, who died in 1819 at the age of fifty-three, had for much of his life been bedridden. Amongst his many achievements the invention of the 'hidden hinge' snuff box was the most important. The knuckles of the snuff box's hinge were formed alternately from the lid and the back of the box, with a metal rod passing very precisely through the centre of the knuckles. This rod was a little shorter than the box so as not to protrude through the ends, which were than 'stopped' with a minute plug in such a way that the mechanism was invisible even on close inspection. However, the manufacture and marketing of this invention was left to Charles Stiven from Laurencekirk, Kincardineshire, (now Grampian), the product being initially referred to as the Laurencekirk snuff box.

The wood used was generally syca-more, which has a very close grain and a pleasing colour. Early snuff boxes were hand-decorated either in coloured paints or in pen and ink work. The finished boxes were then given numerous coats of varnish, which enriched the final appearance as well as protecting the surface. Highly skilled artists were employed in this work, including the well known Victorian watercolourist William Leighton Leitch, who later became one of Queen Victoria's tutors. Favourite subjects for snuff box decoration were coaching scenes, field sports and 'drinking' topics.

By some means, but certainly not by design, the secret of the hidden hinge snuff box found its way to Cumnock in Ayrshire (now Strathclyde), only a few miles from Mauchline. The first manufacturer in Cumnock was William Crawford around 1810. Whether he copied the Laurencekirk hinge from a box brought to him for repair, or not, we may never know for certain, although this does seem a plausible explanation and is the one now generally accepted. Crawford was unable to keep the secret to himself for many years, because by the early 1820s at least fifty separate Scottish snuff box manufacturers are known to have existed, mainly in Ayrshire. These included William and Andrew Smith of Mauchline, whose family had previously been employed in the production of razor hones in the locality.

With so many manufacturers, total snuff box production was considerable but the habit of snuff taking was beginning to decline. It became essential for manufacturers to diversify in order to survive. This was beyond the capabilities of many of the specialist snuff box manufacturers, who eventually went out of business, thereby reducing competition for the survivors, one of whom was W. and A. Smith. However, according to an account of the economy of Mauchline published in 1845 the town possessed a 'very extensive manufactory of wooden snuff boxes. In this work about sixty people are employed, who work ten hours a day, six days per week.' It seems most unlikely that production could have been limited to snuff boxes for so long and the probability is that other items were also being made, although the firm was still mainly known for its original products. This view is strengthened by a report only five years later in the *Art Journal* in which Andrew Smith himself stated that the products of his firm 'now consist of every article which you can almost conceive it possible to make, from postage stamp boxes up to tea trays'.

The first of the 'new' products were tea caddies utilising the remarkable hidden hinge, tea being an expensive commodity, which, like snuff, benefited from being kept in an airtight container. It is said that on marriage female employees of Smiths' Box Works were presented with one of the firm's tea caddies. This was a more generous gift than it may seem because these caddies were expensive items, being beautifully decorated and most skilfully made.

Diagram illustrating how the knuckles of the integral hidden hinge snuff box are formed alternately from the lid and back of the box.

Over the course of the next century Smiths of Mauchline and their few competitors were to produce tens of thousands of articles in hundreds of styles and in several different finishes, selling them in virtually every inhabited location in Scotland and many cities, towns and villages in England and Wales, and with a considerable export market.

Snuff boxes continued to be made, albeit in ever decreasing numbers, well into the 1870s and at least one Smiths' employee possessed the necessary skills to repair damaged boxes into the twentieth century. The invention and development of the hidden hinge snuff box is therefore a vital part of the history of Mauchline ware, without which the fascinating range of beautifully produced items, now sought after by an ever increasing number of collectors throughout the world, would never have been created.

Needle books and boxes. Top: 'Athole' tartan box. 'Seaweed' needle book. Shetland knitter photographic ware needle book. Coloured fern ware needle book. 'Rob Roy' tartan needle box with hand-painted view on top. Bottom: Mons Meg (cannon) Edinburgh Castle. Crystal Palace Terrace, both needle books in transfer ware.

THE PRODUCT RANGE

Since most Mauchline ware items were produced in at least two and very often three or four different finishes it is logical to consider the range of products before dealing with the various types of decoration.

From the 1830s a steadily decreasing number of snuff boxes continued to be made alongside an ever increasing range of needlework, stationery, domestic and cosmetic items as well as articles for personal decoration and amusement. In addition an incredible range of boxes in every conceivable shape and size and for limitless purposes was also produced. Tea caddies and cigar cases were the first of the new lines but by the middle of the century, when the industry was at its zenith, virtually anything which could be produced in wood, was comparatively small and served a useful purpose found its way into the product range.

Needlework items are the most numerous group. Containers designed to house or dispense cottons, threads, silks, ribbons, wool, string, pins and needles were made in many shapes and sizes. Also produced were darning blocks and mushrooms, scissors cases, containers for knitting pins, crochet hooks and bodkins and a remarkable range of novelty thimble containers and tape measures. Amongst the most attractive sewing items are the delightful egg-shaped sewing 'etuis', varying in size from bantam to duck eggs. These eggs, when opened, reveal a hollow dowel with a removable top fixed to the base of the egg and designed to hold needles. A small cotton or thread spool was passed over the dowel and a thimble completed these delightful portable sewing companions.

A large number of cotton, thread and ribbon manufacturers purchased Mauchline ware containers for their products, their names being clearly yet discreetly displayed either inside the lid or on the base. Thus rather mundane necessities were transformed into attractive gifts. Manufacturers known to have used Mauchline ware boxes in this way include J. and P. Coates, Clarks, Chadwicks, Glenfield, Kerr, MEQ and Medlock.

Although W. and A. Smith were so prominent, the Caledonian Box Works in Lanark was another major manufacturer. Founded by a former Smiths' employee, Archibald Brown, in about 1866, this firm supplied large numbers of decorative boxes to J. and P. Coates and no doubt other cotton manufacturers. An indication of the size of this trade can be gained

Pin cushions. Top: Cleft in High Rock, Tunbridge Wells. Grace Darling's tomb, Bamburgh. Royal Crescent, Bath (all in transfer ware). Bottom: Fern ware. Coloured fern ware. Alloway Kirk (transfer ware). Stuart tartan. Abbotsford (transfer ware).

from the fact that the Caledonian Box Works had a contract with the local abattoir for the supply of bone. This was used for the small 'eyes' inserted in the sides of the boxes and through which the cotton or thread could be fed. Archibald Brown was a very keen and proficient photographer and after selling the Lanark company to Mackenzie and Meakle in about 1900 he concentrated on this interest, being responsible for many of the photographic views which subsequently appeared in railway carriages.

Stationery items ranged in size from large blotting folders down to small bookmarks and included cylindrical rulers in great variety, some incorporating a pencil and rubber whilst others were covered in a mass of postal information. Rulers containing rubbers and pencils are instantly recognisable by a small knob at one end for the pencil and a much larger knob for the rubber at the other end. If the knobs are of uniform size it is unlikely that the ruler has any additional facility. Novelty inkwells, pens, pencils, pencil boxes and letter openers were also made as well as many designs of bookmark including a patented combined bookmark and paper cutter.

Boxes were produced for postage stamps of one, two or three denominations, and the single denomination boxes were usually circular. The larger boxes were fitted with 'slopes' to facilitate easy stamp removal. Tartan finished boxes often had a facsimile stamp or even a genuine one glued to the lid. The head of Sir Rowland Hill, the originator of the Penny Post, will be found decorating some stamp boxes.

Although wood is not perhaps the most obvious material for making items of personal decoration, a number of very attractive bracelets, earrings and brooches were produced in Mauchline ware. Some of the bracelets incorporated hand-painted segments suggesting manufacture around or perhaps before 1860. Such items would have been expensive.

The most beautiful and delicate handles were made for ladies' parasols and since gloves were an essential part of Victorian dress glove stretchers were another requirement produced in Mauchline ware. Accessories for the dressing table included ring trees and powder puff boxes as well as clothes brushes and hair brushes. One of the most unusual items recorded in this group is a posy holder,

ABOVE: *'Advertising' containers. Top: Jedburgh Abbey (transfer). Box for six cotton reels commemorating the wedding of Alfred, Duke of Edinburgh, and the Grand Duchess Maria of Russia in 1875 (Caledonia tartan). Ribbon dispenser, Jedburgh Abbey and Abbotsford (transfer). Bottom: 'Classical temple' shaped box with sentimental verse on roof. Black lacquer box, Weymouth view (transfer). Rectangular box, Scott Monument, Edinburgh (transfer).*

BELOW: *The same containers but with the tops reversed to show the names of the various manufacturers for whom the boxes were produced. Top: Clark and Company. Glenfield. Medlock. Bottom: Chadwicks. Clark and Company. Clark and Company.*

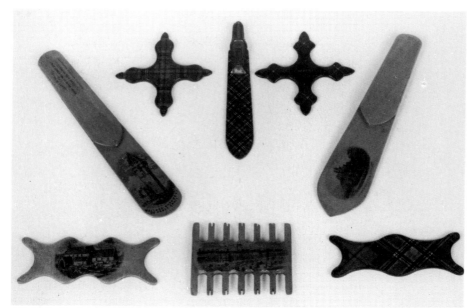

ABOVE: *Bookmarks and silk winders. Top: Bookmark, Wallace Monument (transfer). 'McBeth' tartan winder. Patented 'McBeth' tartan combined bookmark and paper cutter. Winder ('Campbell' tartan). Bookmark, Corfe Castle (transfer). Bottom: Winder, Llanaber church (transfer). Comb winder, Royal Crescent, Weymouth (transfer). 'McLean' tartan winder.*

BELOW: *Stamp boxes. Top left, two-denomination box, Stevenstone House, Torrington (transfer). Top centre, three-denomination box, Weymouth (photographic). Top right, two-denomination box, Burns Monument (transfer). Centre, two-denomination 'drawer' type box in 'Albert' tartan with an actual Queen Victoria stamp. Bottom, single-denomination round box in 'Prince Charlie' tartan and with a facsimile stamp of the creator of the Penny Post, Sir Rowland Hill.*

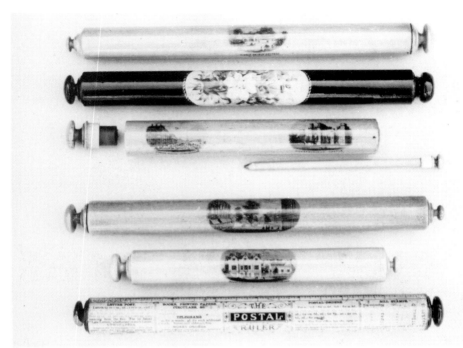

Cylindrical rulers. Top to bottom. Tibby Sheils' Cottage, St Mary's Loch (transfer). Black lacquer with floral decoration. Grand Parade, Eastbourne, and Herstmonceux Castle (transfer). The Promenade, Cheltenham (transfer). Beau Manor, Loughborough (transfer). Postal ruler with Weymouth view on reverse (transfer). The differing sizes of the end knobs indicate that the ruler is hollowed out to hold a pencil and a rubber (see Eastbourne view ruler).

possibly derived from the more common tulip-shaped spill vase. Containers for cosmetics included boxes designed for face powder, rouge, cold cream and lip salve.

The domestic scene was very well catered for, napkin rings being perhaps the most common item of all. They were made in all Mauchline ware finishes and were also amongst the lines produced from relatively early days until the end of production in the 1930s. They will often be found numbered from one to six, having originally formed part of a boxed set. Occasionally rings numbered up to twelve will also be found.

The Victorian breakfast table may well have been graced by a Mauchline ware egg cup cruet although individual egg cups are far more likely to be found by today's collectors. Several versions of egg timers, both free-standing and for wall mounting, were also produced.

Items of more general usage include a wide variety of spill vases and candlesticks. These were made in all the main finishes as well as more costly versions produced from two contrasting woods.

Matches were essential to the Victorian home and a wide variety of match containers was manufactured. Some were no more than novelty matchboxes serving no additional purpose, whilst others incorporated a bone holder for an individual match. Often erroneously called 'go to beds', this type could serve the purpose of a candle providing light for just long enough to get into bed. Their true purpose, however, was to melt sealing wax without burning one's fingers!

Containers for money ranged from ladies' handbags, a tartan ware version being owned by Queen Victoria, and smaller purses through to a massive range of money boxes. Some money boxes are

ABOVE: *Items for personal decoration. Top: Brooch (subject and tartan unknown). Brooch ('McInnis' tartan). Brooch (hand-painted view of Holyroodhouse). Centre: 'Burns' brooch. Tartan cuff-links. Tartan bracelet with hand-painted view of Loch Vennacher. Brooch, Fyvie Cottage Hospital (transfer). Front: Brooch, Burns Monument (transfer). Opening locket containing eleven 'concertina' views of the Isle of Wight (transfer views of Shanklin on the locket itself).*

BELOW: *Egg cups and timers. Centre, Egg cup cruet. Each egg cup has a different transfer view of Stirling. Top left, St Mary's Hall, Cheltenham (transfer). Bottom left, Egg timer, Cardiff views (transfer). Top right, Helensburgh (transfer). Bottom right, Bude Haven, Cornwall (transfer).*

ABOVE: *Napkin rings (the upper ring is described first). 'A Merry Christmas'. Contrasting woods, Lowestoft pier (transfer). Fern ware (Number 4). Fern ware (Number 1). 'Scotland' tartan. 'Seventy-ninth' tartan. Coloured fern. 'McKay' tartan with photograph of Forth Bridge. Wotton-under-Edge (transfer). The Glen, Sidmouth (transfer).*

BELOW: *Some less common items. Top: Ring tree ('McLean' tartan). Spill vase in two contrasting woods, Dalkeith Palace (transfer). Small tankard in two woods with green fern decoration. Below: Glove stretcher in 'Prince Charlie' tartan. Posy holder, the Bowder Stone (transfer).*

13

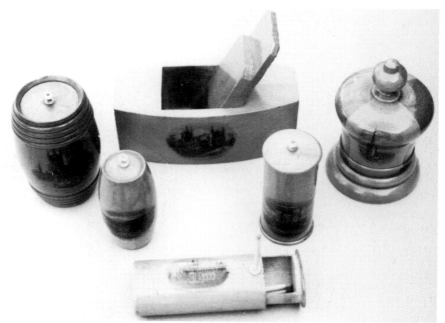

ABOVE: *Match holders, Large barrel, St John's College, Cambridge. Small barrel, Moffat. Miniature plane, St Mary's Church, Rickmansworth. Cylinder, HMS Victory, Portsmouth. Crown, Wakefield Cathedral in two contrasting woods. Foreground: Oval 'slide', Hereford Cathedral. All views are in transfer ware.*

BELOW: *Money boxes. Back, locomotive, The Parade, Skegness. Left, castle, Great Malvern. Centre, chest, Melrose Abbey. Right, cottage, Pevensey Castle. Front, 'trick' money box, West Bay, Bridport. All are in transfer ware.*

UPPER: *Spectacle cases. From top: Martyrs'*
Memorial, Oxford. Queen Square, Bath. Sari
down, Isle of Wight. All are in transfer ware.
CENTRE: *Items associated with card games.*
Back, 'two-pack' card box, Abbotsford and
Melrose Abbey (transfer). Centre, Bezique
scorers; Shakespeare's House (transfer). Fern-
ware. Coloured fernware. Front, Cribbage
scorer, Eastbourne ('Rob Roy' tartan and
transfer). Foreground, Trumps indicator
('McBeth' tartan).
LOWER: *Buttons. A set of nine waistcoat*
buttons in 'scott' tartan.

in the form of chests and castles but an
unusual shape is that of a locomotive.
Trick money boxes were produced and
are generally found either in almost mint
condition, indicating that the young saver
had despaired of extracting his money
and given up trying, or in a very poor
state, where youthful patience has been
exhausted and various implements have
been used as safe cracking tools!

At least three distinct versions of
spectacle cases have been recorded and
the interest in photography is catered for
with picture frames in many styles and
sizes as well as Mauchline ware boarded
photograph albums.

The Victorians were great card players
and this interest is represented by boxes
for one, two or even more packs of
playing cards. Usually these boxes had
three miniature cards glued to the top to
indicate their purpose. Other items
associated with games include cribbage
boards, bezique markers, dice shakers
and Chinese puzzles.

A small circular tartan box with three
minute cards on the lid contains four
black lacquer discs. A small facsimile
card, one for each suit, appears on the
reverse of each disc to indicate which
suit is trumps.

The children were not ignored and
skipping rope handles, tops, pop guns and
whistles will all be found in Mauchline
ware.

There remains one great puzzle. This
concerns the 'Breadalbane' button, or
rather the tens of thousands of these
buttons believed to have been made from
the late 1840s until the early 1850s. Originally produced for the nobleman after
whom they were named, production was
said to have reached twelve thousand

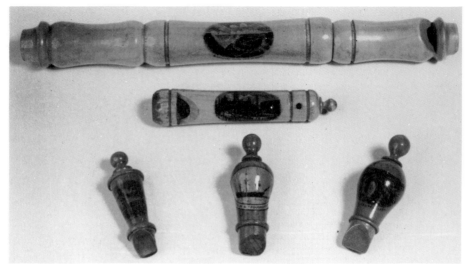

Whistles. Back, Combined whistle and pop gun, Blackgang Chine, Isle of Wight (transfer). Centre, George Square, Glasgow (transfer). Front: The lighthouse, Cromer (transfer). HMS Foudroyant (photographic). The Coupee, Sark, (transfer).

daily at one stage! Victorian buttons have survived in vast numbers and yet relatively few Breadalbane buttons have come to light, although those that have are in good condition. Perhaps an explanation for their puzzling scarcity will one day be found.

This chapter is by no means exhaustive but will give the reader some indication of the vast range of items produced in Mauchline ware during its hundred or so years of manufacture. The following chapters deal with the various finishes applied to these products.

TRANSFER WARE

The precise date of the first transfer-printed wares is not known but they were certainly being manufactured in quantity by the early 1850s and possibly very much earlier, continuing until the effective end of Mauchline ware production in 1933. More items were produced with transfer decoration than in any other finish. Transfer ware was true souvenir ware in that each piece was decorated with a view associated with the place of purchase.

The transfers were applied to the finished articles prior to their receiving several coats of slow drying oil copal varnish. This process was said to take from six to twelve weeks to complete, although it seems certain that accelerated means of varnishing must have been developed to cope with the sheer scale of production. However, this lengthy and

careful process of manufacture must largely account for the extreme durability of these products, many of which have survived in near mint condition.

As with the earlier hand-decorated snuff boxes, the main type of wood used continued to be sycamore, generally known as 'plane' in Scotland, its pale colour making an excellent foil for the darker transfers. Whilst the majority of Mauchline ware items were small, thus warranting only a single transfer, it was by no means unusual for six or even more transfers to be applied to some larger pieces. Where more than one transfer was applied, the views were always related to one another, either by subject or else geographically.

The Scottish home market appears to have been completely saturated. Whilst

16

'Burnsian' views form by far the largest single grouping and views associated with Sir Walter Scott also figure prominently, there can hardly be a location in Scotland which was not recorded. In addition to virtually every town and village, a vast number of beauty spots, country houses, churches, schools, ruins and even cottage hospitals have been immortalised in transfer ware. The remainder of Great Britain was hardly less well represented, although views were in the main of the many seaside resorts and inland spa towns which became increasingly accessible to a growing number of people as a result of the rapidly expanding rail network.

The Isle of Wight was particularly well catered for, possibly because of Queen Victoria's love of the island through her

Larger items often had more than one transfer. This photograph frame has four Northumberland views.

Views associated with Robert Burns and Sir Walter Scott. ABOVE: *Scott Monument, Edinburgh (transfer)*. RIGHT, UPPER: *Burns Monument (transfer)*. RIGHT: *Alloway Kirk (transfer)*.

BELOW, LEFT: *The old village, Shanklin, Isle of Wight. The buildings in this view are virtually unchanged today.*
BELOW, RIGHT: *A Welsh market scene, one of a delightful series of views depicting Welsh rural life.*

ABOVE: *Seaside resorts.* UPPER: *Wellington Crescent, Ramsgate. Carlisle Parade and Robertson Terrace, Hastings.* LOWER: *The new pier, Skegness. A very animated seashore at Llandudno.*

BELOW: *Two heart-shaped pin discs (cushions).* LEFT: *The suspension bridge, Clifton (Bristol) shows Isambard Kingdom Brunel's masterpiece and a train in the left foreground. This is one of very few views to include locomotives.* RIGHT: *The river Avon at Stratford and the Church of the Holy Trinity.*

THE HOLBORN VIADUCT

BLACKFRIARS NEW BRIDGE

ABOVE: *Occasionally a transfer print will help in dating an article. This powder box has a view of the 1886 International Exhibition in Edinburgh.*

LEFT: *These lively London views are on either side of a swivel memorandum tablet.* UPPER: *Holborn Viaduct.* LOWER: *Blackfriars New Bridge.*

residence at Osborne House, itself the subject of transfer views. Each of the popular south and east coast resorts, including Bournemouth, Brighton, Eastbourne, Hastings, Margate, Clacton and Scarborough, was represented with several views. Neither did the Channel Islands escape the attention of the Mauchline ware manufacturers and even Sark, with its tiny population, warranted at least one view, whilst the main islands of Jersey and Guernsey are very well recorded. The ever popular Stratford-upon-Avon was a close rival to London's many places of interest, although some of the capital's most obvious landmarks seem not to have been recorded. Amongst the many inland resorts featured in transfer views are Harrogate, Chester, Bath, Malvern and Cheltenham. Inevitably some less obvious places were recorded, possibly because an anticipated tourist boom failed to materialise. This would account for views of Torrington Station or the New Baths at Croft!

Since transfer ware was produced continuously for some eighty years it is reasonable to assume that there would have been periodic updating at least of urban views to reflect changes of fashion, transport and indeed of the towns themselves. The evidence, however, is to the contrary. New transfers were introduced as more and more places were considered sufficiently commercial, but there is no clear evidence of an earlier view being revised. From the mid 1890s motorised transport became increasingly commonplace but although a great many town and city scenes have been recorded remarkably few views have come to light showing any form of motorised transport. Indeed, railways are as old as transfer ware itself and yet locomotives appear on only a handful of views. This suggests that most of the transfer plates were made before about 1880, with few, if any, being produced after 1890. Although production was to continue for another forty years or so the popularity of Mauchline ware was in decline and the cost of producing a vast number of new plates would perhaps have been prohibitive.

Since the same or similar transfer ware views were used over a long period, they are of little assistance in dating any particular piece. This difficulty is aggravated by the fact that so many lines such

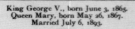

King George V., born June 3, 1865.
Queen Mary, born May 26, 1867.
Married July 6, 1893.

ROYAL FAMILY.
Edward, Prince of Wales, born June 23, 1894.
Prince Albert, born December 14, 1895.
Princess Victoria, born April 25, 1897.
Prince Henry, born March 31, 1900.
Prince George, born December 20, 1902.
Prince John, born July 12, 1905.

ABOVE: *The top of a jewel box, presumably made to mark George V's coronation in 1910.*

ABOVE, RIGHT: *(Upper). The top of a box produced for Queen Victoria's jubilee in 1887. (Lower) The back of the same box.*

RIGHT, CENTRE: *Crayon box with a view of Glasgow Royal Exchange.*

RIGHT, LOWER: *The top of a pin cushion in the form of a three-legged stool. This is of interest because of its view of Mauchline as well as the claim that it was made of wood from the garden of Burns's great friend, Gavin Hamilton.*

as napkin rings, paper knives, rulers, egg cups and memo books were themselves produced in very similar form throughout the transfer ware era.

There are, however, exceptions. A large number of books were produced with Mauchline ware boards. Many carry a publication date and others, especially those purchased as gifts, often have a dated inscription on the fly leaf.

A number of major exhibitions and royal occasions were commemorated with transfer views so that articles so decorated can be very accurately dated. Exhibitions were held in Glasgow in 1861 and in Edinburgh in 1886, the venues of both being recorded by transfer views. Queen Victoria's Golden Jubilee of 1887

21

was a fillip for the Mauchline ware manufacturers, with a wide range of goods celebrating this event with transfer decorations. Probably the last royal occasion to receive this treatment was the coronation of King George V in 1910.

Occasionally a less orthodox form of dating is possible. For example, a 'castle' money box with a lovely panoramic view of Great Malvern contains a slip of paper with the message 'For Mary Selina Badham born Thursday July 2nd 1886 being one penny per week from the date of her birth, from her Aunt and Godmother — Elizabeth Tridman'. Mary Selina's box is in near mint condition suggesting that either she was not particularly thrifty or else, more sadly, that she may have died in early childhood. Another example is a small crayon box with a view of Glasgow Royal Exchange, proudly inscribed as belonging to Maggie Todd of Newlands, Glasgow, and dated 1897. But, for the most part, dating must be speculation based on the 'feel' which is acquired from handling a large number of different items.

Very occasionally a piece of transfer ware will additionally — and in very small print — include a 'publisher's name'. This refers to the name of the retailer and probably indicates a particularly prolific selling agent. The name of C. Maclean or Maclean and Son of Dundalk has been frequently recorded, the Maclean family having been stationers in that town prior to 1911. John Rose was postmaster at Inveraray around 1880 and his name appears on some items depicting the well known local castle. A. and R. Robb are also recorded at Coldstream, where they had a grocer's and newsagent's business towards the end of the nineteenth century. These 'publishers' names' probably appear on no more than one piece in a hundred and are therefore well worth looking for.

Far more common was the practice of disclosing the source of the wood from which the article is purported to have been made. On a 'stool' pin holder it states that it was made from wood grown in Gavin Hamilton's garden. This piece is particularly interesting as the view is of Mauchline's High Street and Gavin Hamilton was a patron of Robert Burns. Other items were supposedly made from wood grown on Flodden Field, on the lands at Abbotsford, on the banks of the Doon or Tweed and even from the Old Gallows Tree at Doune Castle.

PHOTOGRAPHIC WARE

Many items of Mauchline ware are found with photographs applied as a decoration as an alternative to transfer-printed views. These are sometimes referred to as 'stick-on' photographic ware although the prefix hardly seems necessary.

Although photographic ware was probably introduced twenty to thirty years after the first transfer-decorated items, examples will be found of most of the Mauchline ware product range. The obvious exceptions are snuff boxes, tea caddies and cigar cases, production of which had virtually ceased by the time the first photographic ware was produced in the mid 1860s.

The commencement date may well have coincided with the establishment of the Caledonian Box Works in Lanark in 1866. This company was founded by Archibald Brown, who was a very keen photographer and even made his own cameras. He had been employed by W. and A. Smith, who were at the peak of their success at that time, and it seems inconceivable that Brown would have started his own factory in Lanark unless he had some new product in mind. Simply to compete with his old employers by producing identical wares would have been both unimaginative and probably commercially suicidal. It also seems possible that Brown was an acquaintance of George Washington Wilson, perhaps Scotland's best known photographer. Wilson's work was extensively used on photographic ware and it therefore seems likely that Brown, perhaps with the technical assistance of Wilson, had photographic decoration in mind when he started the Lanark company.

It is always very difficult to date items of Mauchline ware with any accuracy but a copy of Sir Walter Scott's *The Lady of*

ABOVE: *The cover photograph on a copy of Sir Walter Scott's 'The Lady of the Lake'. It depicts a group of soldiers at ease on the battlements of Stirling Castle.*

RIGHT, UPPER: *Ventnor, note the bathing machines (photographic).*

RIGHT, LOWER: *Scarborough Castle and the busy harbour (photographic).*

the Lake is very helpful in this respect. The covers are in oak, not the more usual sycamore, and an inscription on the back states that the book was bought in the Douglas Room of Stirling Castle. Many items of Mauchline ware carry the same information. The photograph on its cover shows in great detail a group of soldiers at ease on the battlements of Stirling Castle and is possibly the work of Wilson, who was responsible for the photographs within the book. Whilst it lacks a publication date, the original owner dated the fly leaf, 8th July 1868. This is just two years after Archibald Brown opened his Lanark works and strengthens the probability that this was the commencement date of photographic ware.

Most photographs are of good quality and from a historical viewpoint are of far greater interest than transfer views in that

A jewel box with several interesting features. The large photograph of Ellen's Isle, Loch Katrine, is by George Washington Wilson. The box is also decorated with six smaller transfer prints (two unseen) of the same area and, in addition, carries the 'publisher's' (retailer's) name of C. McLean, Dunkeld. The wood used to make the box is stated as being from the 'Athole Plantations'.

they are factual. However, there are a number with indistinct views and it is likely that any lack of enthusiasm for photographic ware amongst collectors is based on their having seen only these poorer examples.

W. and A. Smith are unlikely to have ignored the commercial potential of this new style of decoration and there is no doubt that they produced similar wares. However, they clearly preferred their more delicate transfer ware and probably dropped their photographic work at the first opportunity. Brown sold his Caledonian Box Works in about 1900 so W. and A. Smith had a monopoly from then on.

Examples will be found of transfers and photographs decorating the same item as well as photographs applied to both fern and tartan backgrounds. Photographic ware was also exported. All recorded photographic ware suggests that the photographs were taken between the 1860s and the very early 1900s.

Napkin rings. (Left) Lion's Head and Signal Hill, Capetown (Photographic). An early motor car can just be seen in this view. (Right) An early photograph of Dunlop Street, Barrie, in Canada.

Three tartan ware items showing the techniques used to disguise joins on curved surfaces with tartan printed paper. The dome shape conceals an ink well ('Campbell' and 'McDuff'). The egg is in 'McBeth' tartan and the parasol handle is in 'Frazer' tartan.

TARTAN WARE

In the early 1840s the inventive Smiths designed an ingenious machine capable of 'weaving' tartan designs on to paper. The machine employed a series of pens, each using a different coloured ink, the result being an accurate representation of the so called authentic tartans.

Before this invention, tartan and plaid decoration was applied directly on to the wooden surface. This process not only required considerable skill and patience but also a vast amount of time, and without the new machine the production of tartan ware might well have been extremely short-lived. As it was, this finish became tremendously popular, not only in Scotland and the rest of Great Britain but also in other countries.

Many Mauchline ware items such as wool holders, egg cups, parasol handles and in particular the egg-shaped sewing companions have rounded surfaces and very great care was necessary in gluing tartan-printed paper to such articles. In theory it is impossible to apply material such as paper to a curved surface without obvious folds or joins. This difficulty was overcome, however, by the application of

black paint to areas where joins would occur, the joins being further disguised by the use of a wavy gold line. Similar care was exercised in matching the tartan design on articles comprising more than one part. So skilfully was this done that it is almost impossible for the naked eye to detect exactly where the parts meet.

The manufacturers stamped the name of the tartan on each product, with the exception of the smallest pieces such as buttons and cuff links. This was always done most unobtrusively in very small gold lettering on a black background.

William and Andrew Smith took the accuracy of their tartan work very seriously. Indeed, they published their own version of *The Tartans of the Clans and Families of Scotland,* a publication consisting of an index of the sixty-nine 'authentic' tartans followed by a sample of each. This is one of very few books published by the Smiths although tartan-covered boards were used by many other publishers, especially for the works of Robert Burns and Sir Walter Scott.

Tartan decoration was applied to virtually the entire range of Mauchline ware

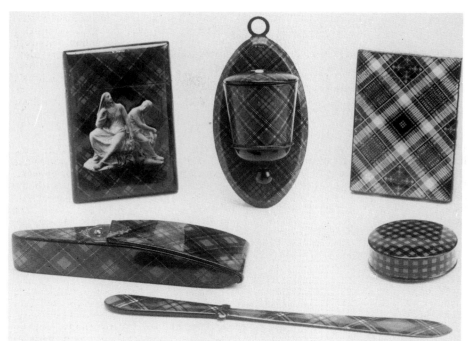

ABOVE: *A selection of tartan ware. Back: Card case with classical figures ('McDonald'). Match holder for wall hanging ('McBeth'). Integral-hinge card case (plaid pattern). Bottom: Case for three pairs of graduated scissors ('McPherson'). Paper knife ('Prince Charlie'). Snuff box ('Rob Roy').*

BELOW: *'Souvenir' fern ware. Match holder with photographic view of Shanklin Castle. Memo book, 'A present from Keswick'. An egg cup from Killarney.*

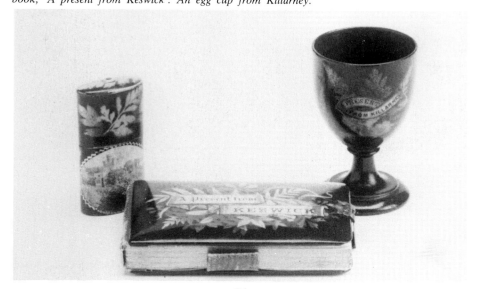

products and its use continued into the twentieth century. However, a fire destroyed their patented tartan printing machine and later pieces were decorated in paper produced by an outside manufacturer. The quality of this paper and also the later workmanship was distinctly inferior, and such items are easily recognised. Even the joins are clearly visible.

Tartan ware was not made exclusively by the Smiths of Mauchline, although they produced the greater part. Davidson Wilson and Amphlet, also of Mauchline, produced tartan ware and Archibald Brown's Caledonian Box Works in Lanark also did so from the mid 1860s.

FERN WARE

It used to be thought that fern ware was a last attempt to revive an industry in decline. However, there is now evidence that the earliest fern-decorated items date from about 1870, when the established transfer and tartan wares were still in great demand.

Fern ware was produced in smaller quantities than the other main finishes and it seems that three, if not four, different processes were used. Almost certainly the first fern ware was produced by W. and A. Smith, although it was also manufactured in Lanark at the Caledonian Box Works. It therefore seems likely that different decoration techniques were employed by these two firms.

In most cases actual ferns were used either directly or indirectly, although one process was a virtual copy of tartan ware, fern-printed paper being used with the telltale gold wavy lines disguising joins on curved surfaces. The majority of fern ware, however, appears to involve the application of various types of fern to the wooden surface, which was then subjected to a dark brown stipple treatment prior to the removal of the ferns and subsequent varnishing.

Whilst transfer and photographic wares were clearly intended for the souvenir trade this can hardly be said of fern ware. Even tartan ware is essentially Scottish, but since ferns occur in many parts of

Fern ware. Back: Napkin rings. Wool or string holder. Hymns Ancient and Modern. Centre: Paper weight. Pin dish. Bottom: Paper knife.

A beautifully made face fan possibly for the French market.

Britain articles in this group would simply have been bought for their undoubted visual appeal. However, some items of fern ware will be found either with an applied photograph or else with a cartouche stating the name of the place of purchase. Fortunately, few examples received this treatment, which hardly contributed to their general appearance.

Although fern ware was a relatively late introduction, a remarkably wide range of wares will be found in this decorative form. Full-size pieces of furniture such as chests of drawers, wardrobes and tables were also produced in fern ware but whether these were made in south-west Scotland or elsewhere is not known.

OTHER MAUCHLINE WARE FINISHES

It is now generally accepted that articles in a number of other finishes but applied to the known Mauchline ware product range have a common origin. Although not always immediately recognisable, these products invariably possess one or two distinct Mauchline ware features. Most numerous are the range of black lacquer ware items which are usually decorated with either a transfer view or a floral design or perhaps a combination of both. An indication of the possible date of these wares is given in a floral decorated notebook, which was apparently a gift to Florence Coombes in 1882. A larger book with a transfer view of Llanwerst church is interesting in that the

weekly diary at the back of the book excludes Sunday — the day of rest!

Perhaps more readily recognisable as Mauchline ware are the somewhat similar 'seaweed' and 'coloured fern' wares. In each case the decoration is applied to the natural sycamore in much the same way as transfer ware. It is difficult to give a firm date to these items although both finishes were also used in combination with transfer decorations. On their own they are clearly gift wares rather than souvenirs and a wide range of items was made in these finishes. The following verse appears on the back of a seaweed card case:

'Oh! call us not weeds, we are flowers

ABOVE: *Black lacquer ware. Back: Dice shaker, Southampton Pier (transfer). Money box, Ramgsate (photographic). Cylindrical container, Winter Gardens, Cheltenham (transfer). Front: Note book, Llanwerst church (transfer). Memo book, dated 1882, (floral design). Box, Clarks' Cottons (pansy design).*

BELOW: *Seaweed and coloured fern. Back: Money box, (seaweed). String dispenser (coloured fern). Needle book (coloured fern). Front: Pin dish (coloured fern). Stamp box (seaweed). Card case (seaweed).*

of the sea,
For lovely and bright and gay tinted are we,
And quite independent of sunshine or showers,
Then call us not weeds, we are ocean's gay flowers!'
Perhaps we should call this finish 'sea flower' ware!

No range of products can be made for more than a century without change and there are other finishes which form part of the story of Mauchline ware. Practically all types were used in combination with other finishes although, to judge by the number of survivors, with only limited success. W. and A. Smith also produced plain white wood articles for home decoration as well as children's wheelbarrows.

THE EXPORT MARKET

William and Andrew Smith of Mauchline and probably one or two other manufacturers enjoyed an extensive export trade, France being the most important European customer. Smiths employed a Paris agent and manufactured some items, including fans, exclusively for the French market. Many French locations, notably Nice and Boulogne, as well as some in Holland, Belgium and even Spain have been recorded with transfer views. The British Empire was an obvious market and Mauchline ware was exported to South Africa, Canada and Australia as well as in large quantities to the United States. It seems likely that the development of some of these markets was associated with emigration from Scotland during the second half of the nineteenth century. The Australian market is thought to have resulted from the emigration of Andrew Smith's daughter shortly after her marriage in 1858.

A group of 'export' items (all in transfer ware). Back: Cotton reel box, Prospect Point, Niagara Falls. Glass holder, Toronto University. 'Saucepan' thimble holder, Schroon Lake, New York. Bottom: Purse, Fontaine des Elephants, Chambery, France. Small box, La Plage, Boulogne. Note book, Bourke Street, Melbourne, Australia.

ABOVE: *An enlargement of the Melbourne view from the note book on the facing page.*

RIGHT: *The beach, Southport, showing one of the first sand yachts? (photographic).*

PLACES TO VISIT

Intending visitors are advised to find out the times of opening before making a special journey. Exhibits at all museums are subject to periodic change so do telephone beforehand to confirm whether the Mauchline ware items are either on display or can be viewed by arrangement. An asterisk * denotes a small collection of local view items.

Abbey House Museum, Kirkstall, Leeds, West Yorkshire LS5 3GH. Telephone: 0113-275 5821.
Baird Institute Museum, Lugar Street, Cumnock, Ayrshire. Telephone: 01290 22111.
Birmingham Museum and Art Gallery, Chamberlain Square, Birmingham B3 3DH. Telephone: 0121-235 2834. The Pinto Collection (Mauchline ware not on continuous display).
Burns House Museum, Castle Street, Mauchline, Ayrshire KA5 5BZ. Telephone: 01290 550045.
Cheltenham Art Gallery and Museum*, Clarence Street, Cheltenham, Gloucestershire GL50 3JT. Telephone: 01242 237431.
Hastings Museum and Art Gallery*, Cambridge Road, Hastings, East Sussex TN34 1ET. Telephone: 01424 781155.
Museum of North Devon, The Square, Barnstaple, Devon EX32 8LN. Telephone: 01271 46747. Collection of fern ware.
Royal Museum of Scotland, Queen Street, Edinburgh EH2 1JD. Telephone: 0131-225 7534.
Towner Art Gallery and Museum*, High Street, Old Town, Eastbourne, East Sussex BN22 8BB. Telephone: 01323 417961.

FURTHER READING

Chapters on Mauchline ware are to be found in many publications, especially those dealing with needlework tools and small antiques.
Furstenberg, Princess Ira von. *Tartanware – Souvenirs from Scotland.* Pavilion Books, 1997.
Pinto, E. H. and E. R. *Tunbridge and Scottish Souvenir Woodware.* Bell, 1970. (Currently out of print.)

CLUB
The Mauchline Ware Collectors Club was formed in 1986. Enquiries should be addressed to the club at: Unit 37, Romsey Industrial Estate, Greatbridge Road, Romsey, Hampshire SO51 0HR.

St Julians Avenue, Guernsey, decorating a book cover. One of many Channel Island views.

ST JULIANS AVENUE GUERNSEY